The Euclid High School Scholars Program

Young Men Changing the Academic Culture in Their School and Community

How They Make a Sacrifice, Make a Difference, and Make History

Willie J. Smith, LSW

Order this book online at www.trafford.com
or email orders@trafford.com

Most Trafford titles are also available at major online book retailers.

Printed in the United States of America.

ISBN: 978-1-4269-3907-5 (sc)
ISBN: 978-1-4269-3908-2 (e)

*Our mission is to efficiently provide the world's finest, most comprehensive
book publishing service, enabling every author to experience success.
To find out how to publish your book, your way, and have it available
worldwide, visit us online at www.trafford.com*

Trafford rev. 10/8/2010

 www.trafford.com

North America & international
toll-free: 1 888 232 4444 (USA & Canada)
phone: 250 383 6864 ♦ fax: 812 355 4082

Acknowledgments

To the MAC Scholars Program of Shaker Heights High School, Shaker Heights, Ohio—for their many years of service to the students of the school district.

To all of those individuals who have provided years of service to our students, especially the African American male population.

Special thanks to Domonique Broome of Euclid, Ohio, for her contribution to this book.

To my mother, Mary Owens, who has the anointing of God upon her, a woman of grace and love, who has given me everything to be the best person that I can be.

To my aunt, Pecola Bowling, who is more than an aunt. She is my other mother in my life.

Finally, to my wonderful son, Joshua Aaron Smith. He is the love of my life and the best son that any father could ever have.

—Acknowledgments

Dr. Joffrey Jones, superintendent of Euclid City Schools District

The Euclid City Schools will become the schools of choice among "first ring" suburbs because we will be recognized for helping all students achieve excellence and readiness for a successful future in the twenty-first century.

The Euclid Board Of Education

It is the policy of the Euclid Board of Education that there shall not be any discrimination on the basis of sex, race, color, religion, age, disability, or national origin in employment or educational programs and activities. Inquiries concerning the application of Title VI, IX, and Section 504 may be directed to the compliance office.

To contact the Board of Education, please call 216.261.2900.

Contents

How It All Started

The story of the Euclid High School Scholars Program began in 2006 with conversations between high school guidance counselors, Karen Brown and Lynn Davis, and intervention specialist, Sharell Benton, who became an administrative principal in 2009. The focus of the conversations was on what interventions needed to be in place to direct African American males into more structured activities that would focus on a positive outreach that the majority of our males would want to be a part of. Several weeks into the school year of 2006, conversation began with Willie Smith, a newly hired family resources manager, who accepted the responsibility to be the advisor to a new program at the Euclid High School. The program would be called the Euclid Scholars Program. The aforementioned women set up the basic structure of the program that would be a program similar to the MAC Scholars program at Shaker Heights High School, in Shaker Heights, Ohio. We received permission from the Shaker Heights City School District to use material from their program to start the scholars program at Euclid High School.

Willie J. Smith, LSW

Dr. Joffery Jones, superintendant of Euclid City Schools District and assistant superintendants, John Schweitzer and John Fell, granted approval to start the scholars program and have provided their unyielding support throughout the years of the program.

Special thanks to the men who serve as consultants, role models, presenters, and mentors to the scholar program, including:

Mr. Steve Hardaway, unit principal/athletic director

Mr. Reggie Echols, industrial department/arts program

Mr. Alan Fletcher, guidance counselor

Mr. Greg James, social studies department/assistant basketball and softball coach

Mr. Carl Jordan, physical education department

Mr. Rashad Wilson, science department/assistant football and basketball coach

Mr. David VanLeer, director of pupil personal

These men present a strong African American male presence at our high school that gives our young men a sense of pride and confidence that they can go to these men for additional support, guidance, and leadership to help them through any personal problems or crises that they might experience. There are many other staff members who have provided help to our program that time and space don't allow me to mention at this time. It is duly noted that our entire high school administrative staff and faculty have been extremely helpful and supportive to the Euclid Scholars Program. I am forever indebted to all of you for providing me with anything and everything that I have ever needed to function as advisor to the Euclid Scholars Program.

Introduction

The Euclid High School Scholars Program, in Euclid, Ohio, began operation in September 2006. Mrs. Karen Brown served as the primary resource and contact person during the beginning stages of the program. We arranged interviews with administrators, faculty, staff, and students to produce a DVD that was made available to the community to introduce our new program and to promote our group. This program started with twenty-four students. The students were selected from the African American male population in grades eleven and twelve who met the grade point average of 3.0 or higher. We wanted to start the program with upperclassmen rather than freshman and sophomores because we believed the group would be better served with the highest grade level students to establish a greater opportunity for leadership and direction. The first goal for the group was to meet the need of improving the graduation rate among African American students in our school. The successful completion of this goal would accomplish another goal of closing the achievement gap between African American and white students in our school.

Another goal was to establish a culture of academic excellence among the African American students in our school. As was mentioned earlier, only twenty-four male students in grades eleven and twelve had achieved a 3.0 GPA or higher. We were very disappointed with such a low number. It became obvious to us that these numbers had to increase if the aforementioned goals were going to be achieved. At our first meeting, the young men had an opportunity to meet and greet each other. To their amazement, they realized that they were a part of a new minority of academic achievers that existed in the school. They were pleasantly surprised that more than half of their group were athletes. All of them were planning to attend college. Many of them were more surprised to discover that they each had a GPA of 3.0 or better. In their associations and interactions, grades were something they didn't talk about. The young men realized that the formation of this group had destroyed the stereotype and myth of the "dumb jock athlete." They had believed that most black athletes were good in sports, but not in classrooms. The group decided to set up a day for group meetings. We decided that Thursday would be our meeting day because it would give us a good start into our weekend. We also decided that it was important to meet during the school day so there wouldn't be any conflicts with afterschool activities, most notably sports practice times. It was important for administration to approve our meeting times during school day to show our group meetings were important enough to allow students to be excused from some classes throughout the school year. The group decided to meet during lunch period rotation so the students would not miss the same class each time we met. It was also decided that a biweekly meeting would be the best arrangement so the students wouldn't miss classes on a regular basis. The group set new goals each year to compliment already existing goals, so there would be something new to accomplish each year. Since 2006, the number of students added to the group has increased. In 2008, the group decided to add sophomores to the group and to add freshman after their first semester in high school. Also, in 2008, the group decided to establish a scholars group in two of our middle schools. In 2009, a scholars group for our second middle school was established. The goals for the middle school groups are very similar to those of the high school group. We wanted both middle school groups to be mirror images of the high school group so the younger students could make easier transitions into the elevated group once they became students at the high school. The middle school group was called YES! for Young Euclid Scholars. Future goals include establishing the scholars programs in each of our seven elementary schools. On group meeting days, the young men are asked to wear shirts and ties. This has provided a sense of pride in group members, as it distinguishes them as members of the scholars program. In 2008, the Euclid Scholars Program adopted the motto, "Make a sacrifice, make a difference, make history." The primary goal in 2008 was to produce, from our program, the first black male valedictorian. In 2009, our third year, the Euclid Scholars Program did make history. The vision and dream became a reality. Mr. Marcus Germany became the first black male student to be named valedictorian of Euclid High School. The accomplishment of his goal has helped members in our group realize that, by hard work and determination, goals can be achieved. The accomplishment of this goal brought even more credibility to our group. We can not only set goals, but we can also achieve goals. In an article in the Cleveland *Plain Dealer* "Metro Section," dated June 9, 2009, Euclid High School was cited among the nation's best high schools for improving the graduation rate among African American students, and the Euclid Scholars Program was mentioned as one of the factors that led to the improvement and the accomplishment of retaining black male students in our high school. The confidence that our members now feel as a result of these achievements has increased their level of self-esteem practically, among our younger members, that our goals can be accomplished in the future, just as they have been accomplished in the past. The students in the middle school programs now believe in the Barak Obama effect, that they can accomplish anything they set out to achieve, including the highest level of office in the world.

The Original Members of the Euclid Scholars Group 2006

- Julius Ayoade
- Christian Black
- Deano Buycks
- Gregory Carter
- Cameron Cofield
- Javier Collins
- Terrell Dumas
- Ryan Fitzgerald
- Donte Hayes
- Alphonso Jamerson
- Anthony Jones
- Chad Lee
- Christopher Lee
- Branden Malone
- Derick McNary
- Donald Murphy
- Cameron Robinson
- Dennis Rodgers
- Tyler Slaughter

- Ethan Smith
- Nathaniel Summers
- Damien Warren
- Walter Watts
- Deion White
- Aaron Wilcoxson

Current Euclid Scholars Group
Members 2009–2010

- Henry Ameyaw
- Ken Amos
- Antoine Alexander
- De'Shaun Boone
- Quincy Brame
- Deonte Brown
- Lakenneth Chambers
- Teddy Cooper
- Quenton Copes
- Anthony Davis
- Di'Jon Davis
- Lorenzo Ellington
- Eon Fawcett
- Julian Ferguson
- Rashid Fitzgerald
- Bobby Gist III
- Antonio Green
- Shaquille Hairston
- Alex Hunter

- Ja'Shan Jabbaar-Hill
- John Jackson
- Terrance Kidd
- Jaylon Lashley
- Ke'Mond Leggins
- Mike Lampkins
- Eric Love
- Byren Malone
- Demario McKenzie
- Darshed Mustafa
- Seth Morgan
- De Marcus Mc Wilson
- Henry Price
- Tommie Pratt
- Jayvon Robinson
- TIshon Rutherford
- Dudley Shepherd
- Christain Simpson
- Darnell Smith
- Kevon Smith
- Lemar Smith
- Zesmenn Spencer
- Paul Styles
- Chris Uzzell

Administrative Staff of Euclid High School

Dr. Charlie Smialeck, administrative principal, Euclid High School

Karen Brown- Guidance Counselor

Karen Brown has worked in the Euclid City School District for twelve years. She presently serves as a guidance counselor but began her career teaching English. She is passionate about encouraging and supporting African American male students to be successful in school and in life. She worked with the REACH program, a middle school program at University High School in Pepper Pike, Ohio for Gifted and Talented African American male students from greater Cleveland, for fourteen years and remains committed to its charter to celebrate the academic talents and success of African American male students and to push them to realize their full potential.

Brown is married, has two young children, and lives in the city of Euclid. She enjoys reading, exercising, watching movies, and spending time with her family.

Two books all African American males should read: *Invisible Man*, by Ralph Ellison, and *The Autobiography of*

Malcolm X. Both books help students grapple with their unique place in our society as African American males and illustrate that, despite societal limitations, it is ultimately up to each of them, as individuals, to determine what kind of men they are going to be.

Quote to live by: "Our deepest fear is not that we are inadequate. Our deepest fear is that we are powerful beyond measure. It is our light, not our darkness that most frightens us. We ask ourselves, who am I to be brilliant, gorgeous, talented and fabulous? Actually who are we not to be? You are a child of God. Your playing small doesn't serve the world. There is nothing enlightened about shrinking so that other people won't feel insecure around you. We are all meant to shine as children do. We were born to make manifest the glory of God that is within us. It's not just in some of us; it's in everyone. And when we let our own light shine, we unconsciously give other people permission to do the same. As we are liberated from our own fear, our presence automatically liberates others." Marian Williamson

Lynn Davis, guidance counselor

Dear Mr. Smith,

I am writing to express the wonderful job done by you with the Scholars Program. This is such a valuable program for our students, and I personally saw incredible, positive changes for many students. Their attitude about education, responsibility, and self-motivation took on totally different importance and value for them. The composition of our school and, of course, the fact that the majority of families consist of one parent, primarily the mother, is another very important reason their Scholars Program must remain. It has gained momentum with each year. It is very heartwarming to see the participants in their shirts and ties spreading the word to those needing help. Keep up the excellent work.

Lynn Davis-guidance counselor

Mrs. Sherrell Benton is the current principal at Glenbrook Education Center. She has been an employee with the Euclid City Schools District for the past ten years and previously worked for the Toledo Public School District. She is happily married and enjoys baking, reading, and working out.

Ghandi said, "Become the change that you want to see." These are words that Mrs. Benton sincerely takes to heart and tries to implement within the school and community environments.

Elizabeth Russo, family resource manager and advisor of Cultural Club Diversity Group

Not Pictured: Angela Flowers, family resource manager

Euclid High School Peer Mediation Advisors

Kathleen McDonald and Leslie Bates

Goals and Guidelines for the Euclid Scholars Program

Role Model—Euclid Scholars are required to be an example of best practices of excellence and behaviors and academic standards. They are expected to set a positive tone with other students in their conversation about what it means to be a positive and appropriate student.

Tutoring Program—Euclid Scholars tutor those who seek academic assistance with school work and life skill issues. These sessions are offered to students before and after school and at lunch periods during the school day.

Recruitment Program—Recruitment to the Euclid Scholars Program can be made by any teacher, staff member, or administrator who refers students to the program for counseling, tutoring, and/or membership. Our most effective recruiting is done by the scholars themselves who may know of students that they can refer who meet the criteria of a 3.0 GPA.

Community Service Program—We believe that is very important for Euclid Scholars to be involved with community service projects. These young men present a positive outreach to the community that presents a level of confidence and support to community leaders and residents.

The Euclid Scholars Group Meetings

High School scholars gather for a photo opportunity
during a scholars meeting

In the first year of the Euclid Scholars Program, we set a goal to promote our group as a viable intervention program to help male students who demonstrated severe behavioral problems and/or academic concerns. The group was presented to our school administration, faculty, and staff to refer students who needed additional support to organize and manage their school day according to school policies. We used our highest academic achieving group members as role models to provide successful techniques for behavior modification and academic achievement. We created a referral form used by the family resources department under the male support group intervention program.

The students that demonstrated behavior problems or needed specialized male support services were referred to Willie Smith, Euclid Scholars advisor and family resource manager, for individual and small group counseling. The Euclid *Sun Journal* newspaper published an article on March 8, 2007 about the Euclid Scholars Program. The focus of the article was to highlight the progress of our group. The article was positive, which provided some much-needed exposure for our group to the community. The article prompted some positive editorial responses the following week. The group went on to become a part of several community organizations—the Euclid Collaborative, a community service referral program, and BRIDGES of Euclid, Ohio. The BRIDGES program was organized by the mayor and city council of Euclid, Ohio. We began to support many community service projects and organized several projects of our own, including the Euclid Youth and Senior Citizen Luncheon Program. We started the program to bring together high school students and senior citizens for lunch to get to know each other and reduce fears that the adults might have of youth, particularly black male youth! The agenda items for this project can be seen in the community service section of this book.

In our second year, we wanted to continue our focus on increasing our presence in our school and community. During our group meetings, we could plan ways to promote our group. Many of our group members possessed entertainment skills and abilities, and they became involved in school plays and the highly popular Euclid Fashion Show. We simply took advantage of every opportunity to showcase and promote the Euclid Scholars Program. The group became larger, and our services to the school and community grew to great success. At the end of our second year, the Euclid Scholars held the first-ever Euclid Teen Summit. The program focused on important youth issues and solutions for a better community. The program drew nearly three hundred youth from the community. The program involved many community leaders, Euclid High School staff, and the Honorable judge Michael Ryan, the youngest black male ever elected and appointed as a Cleveland Municipal Court Judge. He served as our keynote speaker, which brought even more credibility and viability to our program. The Euclid *Sun Journal* provided our program with yet another article promoting the success of our event and explaining how we brought the community together for solutions to many of the problems affecting our youth and community. In our third year, it was brought to our attention that the school could have its first black male valedictorian. Marcus Germany was ranked number one in the class of 2008–2009, and he was a member of the Euclid Scholars Program. It was a goal we wanted to achieve sooner than later. This was a goal that we often talked about when we first organized the program, along with how significant it would be if it was accomplished by a member of our group. The fact that he was the top student in his class gave the members of our group a great deal of confidence we could use for future growth and development. Most importantly, it gave us a greater sense of pride, and we felt that whatever we were lacking in terms of group legitimacy would be accomplished if Marcus Germany became the Euclid High School valedictorian for 2008–2009. The goal of having the first black male valedictorian for our school became a reality in 2008–2009. The young men in our group gained a higher level of confidence and a desire to reach greater academic success and achievement. In 2009-2010, we had the top-ranked sophomores and freshman in the respective classes become members of our group. Obviously, their goal is to become valedictorian at the time of their graduation. Ironically, Marcus' accomplishment occurred in the same year that senator Barak Obama became the first black male to become president of the United States of America. During the time of the presidential campaign and elections, we talked about the irony of both Barak Obama and Marcus Germany making history in the same year.

The Barak Obama effect became our theme in our meetings throughout the school year. "Yes, we can! Conceive, believe, and achieve!"

The goal of our meetings going into our fourth year was to organize a speaker bureau that we could select from to come to our group meetings to teach us ways to become successful adults and entrepreneurs. We wanted our students to become the "next one" to create and manufacture. We brought in speakers once each month (every other meeting). We wanted to know the rules in society of what it takes to be successful. We received great insight from the speakers; they inspired and motivated us to continue on the path of greatness and success. The speakers presented ways of dealing with the struggles and possible rejection students might receive as black males and successful young men. The lessons were invaluable, and our young men got to meet young quality men who could set goals and accomplish them. We believe our group meetings work well for us because each year we set goals on a different focus, without losing the accomplishments of the past. A different focus challenges the young men to a greater sense of responsibility, growth, and achievement. The group meetings provide an opportunity for our group members to bond and establish quality relationships.

The Euclid Scholars meetings are where we come together, a place to grow, develop, and plan our futures, a place where we all belong.

Euclid Scholars Pledge

I am a strong, young, African American man.

I strive to be the difference by upholding the qualities and characteristics as a responsible individual.

I will break the stereotypes by excelling academically and upholding moral standards.

We must come together and make ourselves and our communities better.

We no longer have to stand alone because united we stand, divided we fall.

Euclid Scholars Code of Conduct

Responsibility, Respect, Academic Excellence

1. I will make a conscious effort to always conduct myself in keeping with the goals of the Euclid Scholars Program. Those goals are:
    *   **Responsibility** for my actions and their resulting consequences
    *   **Respect** for self and for others
    *   The pursuit of **academic excellence**

2. I will refrain from voicing any negative comments about the character, reputation, background, or personality of others. I will do this by realizing that if I would not like to hear the same said about me, I should not say it about another person.

3. I will make it a priority to attend all scheduled ESP meetings.

4. I will respect the opinions of others and their rights to voice them without fear of ridicule.

5. I will offer help if I am able and seek help when I need it.

Euclid Scholars Evaluation Form

How long have you been a Euclid Scholar? _____

How did you hear about the Euclid Scholars Program?

_____

How much has the group helped you throughout the year? **Circle one**

None/Some/Great deal

Do you think the group is helpful to other members of the group? **Circle one**

None/Some/Great deal

Would you recommend the group to other students at Euclid High School? **Circle one**

Yes/No

Describe the most effective part of the group and some of the things that impacted you the most.

_____

_____

Describe the least effective part of the group.

_____

What recommendations do you have for the group next year?

_____

_____

Community Service Projects

Agenda for Youth/Senior Citizen Luncheon*

11:15 am (5th period) Leave Euclid High School

11:30 am Arrive Senior Citizen Center

11:45 am Groups organized and luncheon activities begin

* Each student will have one or two senior citizens to whom they will serve lunch. During the lunch period, you will then interview them. After the interview, they will interview you.

Suggested questions to ask and topics to discuss:

* What is your name?

* Where were you born?

* Where did or do you go to school?

* How long have you been a resident of Euclid?

* A favorite memory that you want to share

* The best job you ever had

* Your favorite place to go

* Your favorite thing to do

* Your favorite TV show

* One thing you would like for youth to do **to help you or to help the community**

* What would you like to talk to youth about that would help make Euclid a better place to live for all Euclid residents?

12:40 pm Closing remarks

12:45 pm Return to Euclid High School

Euclid Teen Summit:
Awakening the Social Consciousness of Youth

In partnership with: **BRIDGES**- Bridging Community Connection of Euclid.

Euclid Board of Education- Euclid High School-Forest Park & Central Middle School

Saturday, March 29, 2008- Shore Cultural Centre, 291 East 222nd Street. Euclid, Ohio **8:00am -2:30pm**
*Euclid High School PEP BAND & DRUMLINE
Informational Workshops* Exhibitions *Breakfast& Lunch * College Step Show
*Student Panel Discussions **Participation is free**. Register now for early selection.
*Contact Willie Smith-Euclid High School, (216) 797-7887 (Cell) (216) 254-3177

Saturday Workshops

*Dating /Relationships

(Top 10 ways of maintaining a healthy relationship)

*Conflict Resolution

A Bullying Prevention Program

*Hiv/Aids Awareness

The causes and prevention of Hiv/Aids

Stress/Anger Management

Learn techniques to handle stress and anger positively

*Diversity and Acceptance

Teaching tolerance, exploring race, gender and sexual orientation issues

Tobacco Usage

Tobacco Myths Realities

*Youth Survival Skills

Living in a dysfunctional amily

*DIVA-Girls 2 Women

(Rights of Passage Program)

*Hip Hop and Culture

The history of Hip Hop and impact on today's society

*Men Talk

Leadership skills and ways to avoid negative influences for the adolescent male student.

*Keeping it Real (Storytelling)

Storytelling as a positive influence and (**gossip**) and the negative impact it has on ourselves and others.

Euclid Teen Summit
Tentative Agenda

Saturday, March 29, 2008- Shore Cultural Center
8:30am Registration/Continental Breakfast
9:00am Welcome/Announcements/Speaker-TBA
9:45am Session one workshops
10:35am Break
10:45am Session two workshops
11:35am Break
11:45am Session three workshops
12:30 pm Lunch
1:15pm Afternoon workshops
2:05pm Break
2:15pm College Step Show/High School Dance Teams
3:15pm Closing Ceremony (Charge to Change)
3:30pm Dismissal

Targeted Audience

The students invited will be grades 7-12, with the majority of the 7th and 8th grade students coming from Forest Park and Central Middle Schools. A cross section of area high schools will be invited to attend the program.

Special Needs

*** Workshop presenters may require a fee for their services, however most presenters will volunteer their services. We would like to get continental breakfast Saturday morning donated by area merchants. We would like to provide a free box lunch and would need some suggestions of how to accomplish this goal. We will need to hire security personnel and would need to find funding for this part of our program. We have asked the Euclid

Camber of Commerce to publicize this event. We would like for Channel 22 to publicize and provide television and video coverage for this event.

We will petition funds from the following sources:
Euclid City Schools- Board of Education
Euclid City Hall (Mayor's Office)

Euclid Scholars attend City Club Forum of Cleveland, Ohio 2008

Left to right: Jaylon Lashley; Dr. Robert Franklin, keynote speaker and president of Morehouse College of Atlanta, Georgia; Willie Smith, advisor; and Cortez Bogard

Euclid Scholars Top Honors Award

Presented to Brian Steele 2009

Willie J. Smith, LSW

Euclid Scholars Honors Award Top Athlete

Presented to Kenneth Amos 2009

Euclid Scholar Highest Honor

Presented to Will Smith 2009

Pictured with advisor Willie Smith

Marcus Germany

Ultimate Scholar

Valedictorian, Euclid High School 2009

**First black male valedictorian in the history of the
Euclid High School**

Central Middle School YES! (Young Euclid Scholars Program 2009–2010)

Willie J. Smith, LSW

YES! (Young Euclid Scholars, Central Middle School, Euclid, Ohio)

Mr. Charles Rivers, Ms. Kendra Reddick, Mike Mennel, administrative principal.

Euclid Scholars share a moment at Central Middle School with members from the YES! program during a scholars' meeting.

Central Middle School YES! Induction Ceremony

May 6, 2010

Forest Park Middle School, Euclid, Ohio

Administration Principal Tina Elliott

Assistant Principal Ariel Townes

Not pictured: Assistant principal and YES! Advisor Judy Mc Elroy

Willie J. Smith, LSW

**Euclid High School scholars discussing important
issues with Forest Park YES! members**

**Euclid High School scholars attend a group meeting
with Forest Park YES! members**

Euclid High School scholars attend Forest Park YES! group meeting

Forest Park YES! Induction Ceremony 2008

Getting to Know the Scholars
Lessons Learned ... Lessons Taught!

Marcus Cleveland Germany

First and foremost, I must say that God is the head of my life. Without Him, I don't know where I'd be today. It is with his constant blessings that I am even alive and well today. If I had one thousand tongues, I still couldn't thank Him enough for what He's done for me. I love Him because He loved me first.

I was born in Cleveland, Ohio, on January 19, 1991. My parents are Howard and Brenda Germany. I have one brother and two sisters. Still living, I have my maternal grandmother and great-grandmother, as well as a step-grandfather. They all have supported me endlessly in all of my endeavors. I have three nephews and a niece whom I adore. I also have a host of cousins, aunts, and uncles and others whom I love just as much.

After high school, I plan on attending the University of Cincinnati. I would like to major in pre-medicine. Though I am not sure of which medical school I want to attend just yet, I have decided to be a pediatrician.

I am very involved academically; math and history are favorite subjects. I tutor in math. I am a member of the AIID Student Leadership Team, the EHS Campus Governance Team, and the National Honor Society. I am member of the Euclid Scholars Team, too.

I work at the Euclid Public Library. When I am not working or at school, I enjoy sleeping and chillin' with friends. I also like to go to the movies and bowling. My favorite movies are Tyler Perry/Madea movies, *ATL*, *Death Race*, and *The Bucket List*. I am a huge sports aficionado. My favorite teams are the New York Giants, the Boston Red Sox, and the Houston Rockets. Some of my favorite athletes include Manny Ramirez, Tiger Woods, Tracy McGrady, and Peyton Manning. As far as music goes, I enjoy hip-hop and R&B; gospel and classical soul top my list as well. I love old church hymns. My all-time favorite food is homemade macaroni and cheese. No one makes it like my mom.

Inspirational quotes from some inspirational people:

"In the long run, men hit only what they aim at." —Henry David Thoreau

"Lots of people want to ride with you in the limo, but what you want is someone who will take the bus with you when the limo breaks down." —Oprah Winfrey

"Ability is what you're capable of doing. Motivation determines what you do. Attitude determines how well you do it." —Lou Holtz

"One man cannot hold another man down in the ditch without remaining down in the ditch with him." —Booker T. Washington

Branden Malone

Inspirational quote: "It's not who you are deep down inside that defines you, it's the things that you do." Self quote by Branden Malone

Family: Mother, Lorene Malone; father, Charles Brownlee; brother, Bryen Malone; sisters, Whitney Brownlee, Sandra Brownlee, and Charla Brownlee

College: Morehouse College

Short-term goal: To increase my GPA by .4 points

Long-term goal: To open a successful, upscale, night club and a homeless community center

One thing that would make the world a better place: If all people were less selfish and helped others more

For black males to be successful: I think black males must set and follow their own paths to be successful. By this, I mean we do not need to let are social settings, environments, or any other outside factors determine our actions.

"Nobody can give you freedom. Nobody can give you
equality or justice or anything.
If you're a man, you take it." —Malcolm X

"If you can't find nothing to live for, you better find
something to die for." —Tupac
"A man who stands for nothing will fall for anything."
—Malcolm X

Kevin Muhammad

My name is Kevin Muhammad. I was born and raised in
Cleveland, Ohio. I grew up on East 70th and Hough, where
I watched friends I grew up with fade away or throw away
their lives. Don't get me wrong, I love being down there
because there is love down there. Everyone I visit tries to
keep me level-headed and really doesn't want me doing
what they were doing. They also told me to stay in school,

and I should've kept playing sports. The words I hear the most from people are: "Kev, don't do this street stuff" or "Kev, this street stuff isn't where it's at, man." I have five sisters, two step-brothers, and a step-sister. They all work on driving me crazy and also making my life better. If it weren't for my mom and my step-dad's relationship, I wouldn't be the man I am now. A lot of people don't have good relationships with step-parents, but I am blessed. God has blessed me because one of my most influential people is my biological father. He stays in my life even though he doesn't have to. My dad is there whenever he can be; he can buy me everything, but his conversation saves me. I am thankful for my mom staying strong with six kids, raising us all to stay out the streets and go to college. My mother is the backbone of our family. I am most thankful that God let me be born with a chance and a great family. My main goal right now is to get accepted into the University of Akron. I want to go to college to set myself up for a career in investment banking. I hope to be able to live life as stress-free as I can and be successful

I chose those similar quotes because they're words that I've chosen to live by, ways to remind myself of what it means to be a man. You have to be a man to live in this world, today as well as always.

Lamar Smith

"Treasure life one day at a time, and you will have
success as the reward."
Self quote by Lemar Smith

My name is Lamar Smith, and I was born in Cleveland,
Ohio, on February 13, 1992. I grew up in a home with
a single parent. My mother raised me to be strong and
to strive to avoid failure. My father wasn't around me
all the time, but it only made me stronger as a young
man because I knew, even though I didn't have a male
inference, I was able to know what was the right thing to
do. My goals in life are to help people who have problems
that are affecting them believe that, even though things
may seem bad, there is always hope and it will get better.
Life is the best thing in the world to me. I got a lot of great
things going for myself. My treasure I am proud of is that
I'm an excellent big brother to my sister Layla, which is
getting me prepared for fatherhood in the near future.

Another prize that I'm proud of is that I have a great support system behind me because without support and love from others, I don't know where my life would end up.

I would inspire people by showing them that you can get far in life by being yourself and believing in yourself. Another important factor I would like to get out to people is that leadership plays a big role in every person because you are your own leader with the choices that you make and the words that come out of your mouth, which can determine what type of person you are and the way you present yourself. I would also like to encourage people that if you want something in life, you have to work hard, show effort at all times, and never doubt yourself or give up in anything that you want to accomplish in life. Most of the young people are a joy of happiness because they get a chance to share what they learned in their life to help someone else.

Jayvon T. Robinson

"Nothing is ever out of reach, especially when you have long arms."

My name is Jayvon T. Robinson, and I'm currently fifteen years old. I was born in Cleveland, Ohio, on August 17, 1993. I'm a sophomore attending the Euclid High School. I am enrolled under the Academy of Intellectual and Interpersonal Development small school. I live with both of my parents, as well as two siblings, a younger brother and younger sister. I first moved to Euclid when I was younger, around the age of three. My hobbies and interests are spending time with my friends. I love to laugh, and they are just the people to brighten up my day and make that happen. We hang out at a lot of different places, specifically at the movies, because I have developed an insane habit of collecting movie tickets. But I never neglect sitting back and relaxing by myself once in awhile. I'm not the biggest sports fan, but I like to ski, snowboard, play football, tennis, and golf, and occasionally swim. I also enjoy traveling. I haven't been to many places, but it's always fun to vacation someplace new. I'm a type of person who likes keeping busy; otherwise, I would be overcome by laziness and sleep the day away. So I am a proud and active member in the high school's culture club, conflict mediation, audio visual club, digital production club, and, of course, Euclid Scholars Group. Other interests of mine also include writing my own short stories, novels, and poetry. Regretfully, very few of my many stories are actually completed, and I wish to see them all finished and published one of these days. Although I want to see all my work published, I do not wish to pursue a career in writing.

My ultimate goal in a career is becoming a marine biologist. I plan to study marine biology, marine science, engineering, ecology, and evolutionary biology at some prestigious college, but I would highly prefer Ohio State University, Florida State University, Michigan State University, or the University of South Florida. Eventually, I would like to permanently live in Florida after I graduate from college. What's interesting about being a biologist is the massive amount of work and responsibility involved to obtain such a goal. It's truly an intimidating challenge to face, but the outcome will be worth it. It's a long, rough path to walk down, but I have to always remember to take one step at a time. Studying marine biology isn't my only "passion" in life. I feel that as an individual, just as everyone else, I can make a huge difference in this world. It only took and/

Willie J. Smith, LSW

or takes one person to start the ideas of bias, prejudice, racism, terrorism, and hatred for one another; thus it only takes person to end it all. Somehow, in a way, I truly intend on being that person. I hope and pray that one day I will finally reach all of my dreams and achieve my goals, with the thanks to everyone who aides me along the way.

John Jackson Jr.

I attend Euclid High School. I am a sophomore. I play football, and I also do inside and outside track. I'm also apart of the Euclid Scholars Group—a group of young, African American men who discuss different topics and do different things in the community. This is my first year participating in the Euclid Scholars Group. It is a fun experience, and what makes it even more fun is the man who's over it. This is Mr. Smith, who has been through the ups and downs to become the man he is today. He uses the quote that I like, which is from the famous "I have a dream" speech by Dr. Martin Luther King Jr.: "We should stand together as brothers or perish as men." I will never forget that quote. Another quote I like and will never forget is "Life is not about finding yourself; it's about creating yourself." I have four brothers and one sister. I live with my dad and step-mom, who have created a wonderful home for me, love me deeply, and provide for me very much. And by their love, that is the reason I am able to stand on my own and own up to my responsibility as a young man today. I will continue to be the best that I can be in everything I do.

Christopher Prayear

Hi, my name is Christopher Prayear. I am seventeen years old. I am the middle child of three. I have a sister, Brittney, who is twenty-one years old. I also have a brother, Martell, who is fourteen. I was raised by my mom until the age of eleven; then my father returned into our lives. I would say I had a pretty rough childhood, but there is always someone who had it rougher. Pretty much my entire childhood life I sat back and watched my mom struggle to raise my sister and me. I was blessed to have a strong and very amazing mom as a role model. I would say, for the most part, I was a pretty good child, but I was definitely no angel. As soon as I got to high school, everything seemed to start to go down hill. I mean smoking marijuana, drinking alcohol, bad grades. I was just falling apart. My biggest problem was I had goals, but my foolish behavior was preventing me from fulfilling them. Every time I got high hopes and got my mind in the right state, I would just pulled back down. Unlike most, I was destined to reach my goals. I was destined to break these bad behaviors.

"Every man has potential, but only a man serves a purpose."
Self quote by Chris Prayear

Clarence Hood

Achievement—what is achievement? There is no answer. Achievement changes with whoever you are. Nobody can measure goals; there is no definition to our destiny. Achievement is not a milestone that the world waits for you to hit. It is our passion, our interpretation of happiness, our game-winning shot. There could only be one way to look at achievement: to look at what you want through your own eyes and decide if that is what completes you.

Christian Uzzell

Hello, my name is Christian De'von Uzzell. I am currently seventeen years of age. I was born July, 21, 1991. I am currently in the twelfth grade, and I attend Euclid High School. While attending Euclid, I was lucky enough to become a member of Mr. W. Smith's prestigious scholars program. Here is a little about me: I have many hobbies, which include playing sports and listening to music. My greatest talent is writing poetry. I am ambitious, a pretty determined person, funny, and intelligent. I live at home with my mother, Melody Roscoe; my father, Johnny Roscoe; younger sister, Tierra Fox; and older brother, Cornelious Strickland. My goals include going to college, preferably Baldwin

Wallace, becoming a divorce lawyer, and owning my own family business. My quote for 2009 is "Failure is nothing but a thought that should make you work harder for success." Self quote by Christian Uzzell

Conclusion

The young men in the Euclid Scholars Program have provided the Euclid City Schools District with the chance to see young men serve their school and community with outstanding character, dignity, style, and grace. Some of the young men weren't perfect; some had their own personal issues and concerns during our four years of existence, but as a whole, overall, the program has brought a sense of pride and a belief throughout our school that goals can be accomplished, dreams and desires can be achieved, and "hard work will always conquer talent when talent doesn't work hard." The administration, faculty, staff, and community now realize that a group of young men made every effort to be the best that they, though not perfect, could be, academically and behaviorally. The program at core is focused on deliberate intent that it be a positive, viable intervention program, designed to help every black male in our school and community. However, our main focus was to highlight the accomplishments of young men who were doing good work, doing what was expected of them, and to bring about positive attention to a group of young men who deserved it. There are so many intervention programs that are targeted toward students who demonstrate an unwillingness or inability to perform at their best behaviorally and academically. The Euclid Scholars Program wanted to focus on "positive behavior supports" for students who were in compliance with school rules and policies and serving as the appropriate role models for all students.

I have personally heard young men walking down the halls of our school, talking about their desire to be in the Euclid Scholars Program. These young men were unaware that I was behind them as they walked the hallway to class. What was interesting was that these men challenged each other to become better students so that they could be selected to become members of the program. There are other stories from members of our group who have had similar conversations with students about their desire to become a member of the Euclid Scholars Program. This is just a small sampling of the impact our program has made on the academic culture in our school. I want to apologize for not being able to mention every young man that has been a part of our program. The young men listed represent the original members from 2006 and members in our fourth year, 2010. The young men who weren't mentioned aren't any less important, but time and space forbid that all members be mentioned in this publication. Young men who have been a part of the Euclid Scholars Program, you know who you are, and I know that you will never forget the pride and honor that you received being a member of the group. I personally want to thank every young man that was a member of the Euclid Scholars Program. To all of the

Willie J. Smith, LSW

Euclid Scholars, wherever you are, you truly made the sacrifice; you made a difference, and you made history. "May the Lord watch over you and keep you and may his countenance shine upon you and give you peace." AMEN!

Willie J. Smith

About The Author

Willie J. Smith is a licensed social worker for the state of Ohio. He attended East Technical High School in Cleveland, Ohio, where he played on the football and baseball teams. He received a football scholarship to attend Morgan State University in Baltimore, Maryland. He later transferred to Hiram College in Hiram, Ohio, and earned a BA in social sciences. Willie attended graduate school at Abilene Christian University, where he earned his MS in educational psychology. He has completed some post-graduate courses at Cleveland

State University and plans to earn a PhD in psychology. His previous work experience includes fifteen years in the Cleveland Heights/University Heights School District where he worked as the home/school liaison and house coordinator. The job duties included, but were not limited to, assisting unit principals with student discipline, attendance, and truancy. He served as an assistant football and track coach for the Cleveland Heights High School and coadvisor to the popular and effective Black Male Support Group. The group brought rival group/gang members together to provide interventions to help them resolve group conflicts and then to become positive leaders in the school and community. He served as the diversity and multi-cultural coordinator for the school district and as advisor to the nationally renowned Unity Group at Cleveland Heights High School. Willie worked at Beech Brook Center for the families and children in Cleveland, Ohio, for three years. He worked in the school-based counseling program that served at-risk students and families for the Cleveland Metropolitan School District. He currently works part time at Bellefaire JCB Residential Childcare Services. He has just completed his fourth year as family resource manager for the Euclid City School District. His duties include, but are not limited to, individual and group counseling for at-risk students in need of specialized services. The counseling services are for, but not limited to, academic underachievers and students with attendance and truancy problems. Smith is also a life skills instructor for special education programs at the high school and middle schools. He does group counseling for students involved in inappropriate group activities that could lead to gang involvement, and he is advisor to the highly acclaimed Euclid Scholars Program.

Willie Smith can be contacted through the Euclid City School District, Euclid, Ohio

via e-mail at wsmitty22@yahoo.com or wismith@euclid.k12.oh.us

www.ingramcontent.com/pod-product-compliance
Lightning Source LLC
Chambersburg PA
CBHW031301280526
45784CB00004B/1943

* 9 781426 939075 *